TO

From

Date

<u>Note</u>

Tips To Bring Your Coloring To The Next Level
First of all, pick coloring tools:

You can use pens, markers, pencils, or crayons. Choose whatever you like in terms of texture and feeling. If I would do recommend, here it is. I'd go with pencils for beginner. If you are wanting to play with some advanced techniques or detail work, then go with a set of pencils and a set of markers. Then of course you can throw in pens, crayons, lead pencils, and more later.

Palette/Theme or Better to pick a concept:

Picking color palettes is not easy. I used to spend more than an hours to see professional talk about this. Thus, I recommend making it easier on yourself by using available color palette online. You may search it very easy from Pinterest or use design-seeds website. You will get much more idea to make your artwork great and special.

Finally:

Just do it and let loose. Coloring is an effective stress management and meditation. Let coloring be your calm and have a great

fashion

Note

<u>Note</u>

Fashion

<u>**Note**</u>

<u>Note</u>

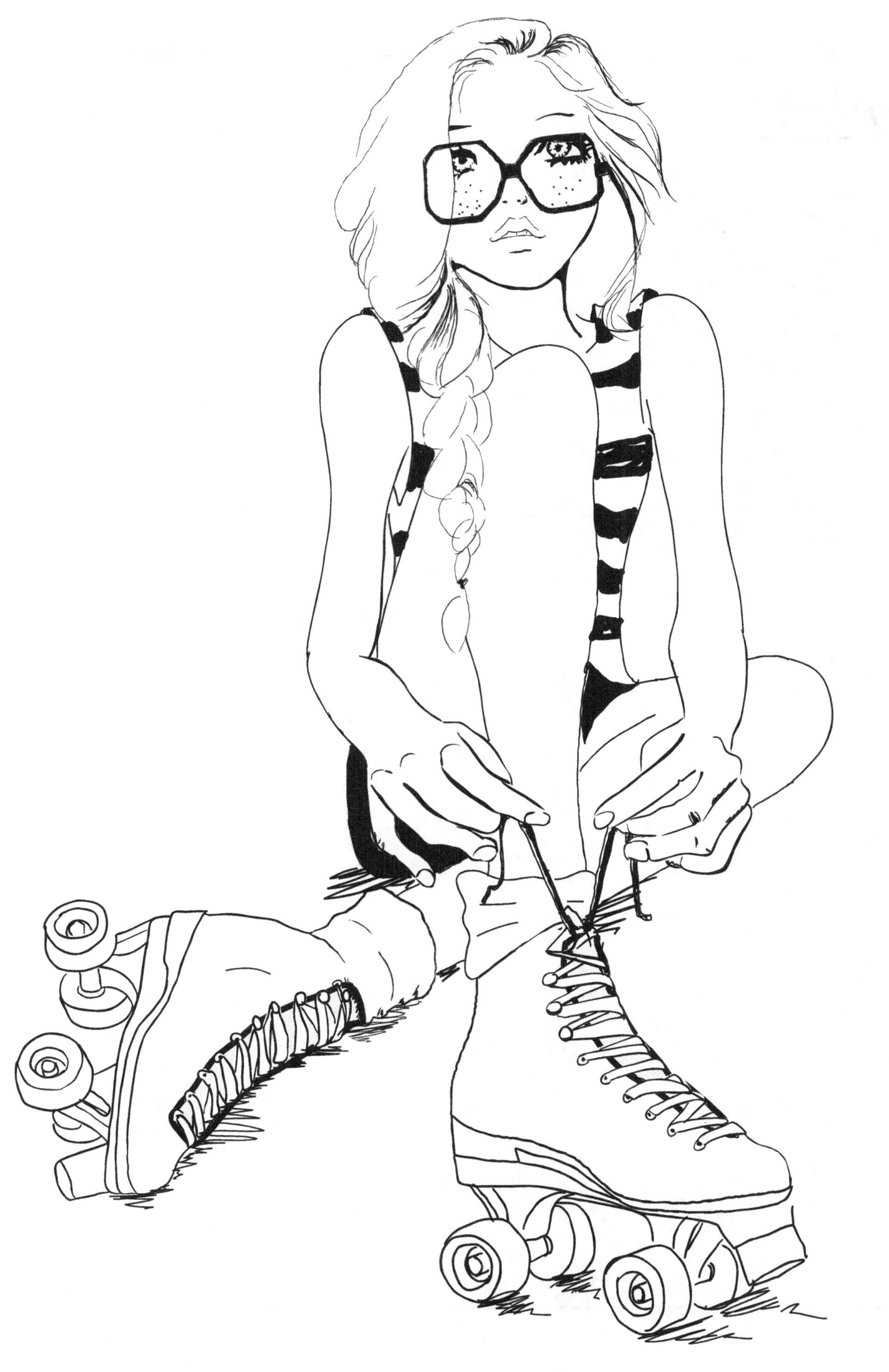

<u>**Note**</u>

Note

<u>Note</u>

Washington Tigers
W
Road to the Championship

<u>Note</u>

<u>Note</u>

BYE
DLC 96

<u>Note</u>

<u>Note</u>

SLUGS,
SNAILS'
& PUPPY
DOG
TAILS

<u>Note</u>

<u>Note</u>

love

<u>**Note**</u>

80

<u>Note</u>

<u>Note</u>

<u>Note</u>

<u>Note</u>

MAKE SOMEONE
Smile

<u>Note</u>

<u>**Note**</u>

<u>**Note**</u>

<u>Note</u>

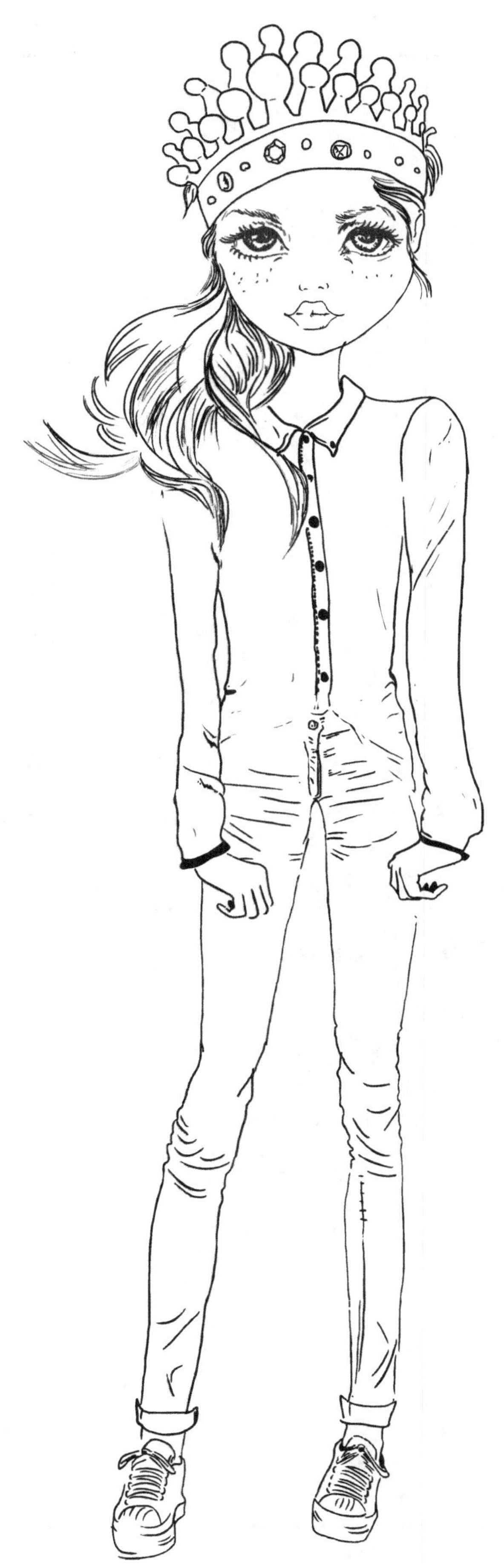

<u>**Note**</u>

<u>Note</u>

fashion